My Little Book of Poetry

by Joy Simons

My Little Book of Poetry

Published by Glorybound Publishing, Camp Verde, Arizona
SAN 256-4564
Printed in the United States of America
1st Edition
KDP ISBN 9798366506489
Copyright data is available on file.
Simons, Joy 1957-
My Little Book of Poetry/Joy Simons
Includes biographical reference.
1. Poetry
I. Title

www.gloryboundpublishing.com

My Little Book of Poetry

by
Joy Simons

Glorybound Publishing
Camp Verde, Arizona
in the year 2022

Don't look for a table of contents. This is much too short. Think of this as something your child would bring home from fourth grade and, smiling with pride and confidence, present to you while you're cooking dinner.

Hands full of whatever food you're chopping, you "Ooh" with pleasure and gingerly take a corner between your pointer finger and your thumb.

"I'll read it later."

You put it aside to preserve it from your cooking mess, but your child looks down and shuffles away in disappointment.

Not that I want you to read it right away, but. . .

When I was young, I wrote poetry. My emotions splashed onto the page in verses of heartfelt angst, but it didn't make the poems good. In fact, I found a notebook lovingly cherished through the decades that held the sacred verses. It was terrible. Don't know what I was thinking.

At lunch with a writer friend, we bemoaned the fact that no-one we knew wrote poetry. After a short discussion, we both agreed to write a few poems and take them to the next peer review. (You know, "If they're not going to do it, why don't we?") When I got home, I remembered the purple prose of my youth. Oh no. Don't know what I was thinking.

I decided to spend an afternoon listening to poetry contest winners of the last five years or so to get my footing. It was terrible. Don't know what they were thinking. My first poem of this stage of my life follows from that experience.

Eulogy for Poetry

I Think that I shall never see
A poem as lovely as a tree.
The poems today are from "the hood"
Words I have never understood.
Where is the rhyme? Where is the song?
Where is the thought behind each long
Awaited word? I want to hear
Beautiful sounds drop in my ear

Can someone please tell me how
Poems came to be
Collections of swearing rhyme?

There once was a woman on stage
Who shouted out lists in a rage
With no rhyme and no reason
She heaved all her words on
Us. Nonsense for page after page.

There once was a man . . . who called himself a poet and proceeded to tell stories of his grandfather in prose. No element of poetry. Just a narration of his life. I don't know where his introduction ended and his performance began, but the audience clapped and cheered when he finished. Is this man a poet or a storyteller? (Don't say both. I know poems can tell stories, but they have to be *poems* my friend.)

I know there are poems with no meter
But the rhyme and the beat are
Still there. Its free-flowing style and fleeting rhyme
Challenges your ear to find the time,
The rhyme is the thing.
This I like.
The slow hike
Of words across the paper.
Tones caught before they escape, or
Moments that make you sigh. . . . .

I think a tree's a lovely thing
With branches and leaves, and everything
It needs to live a prosperous life.
Serenely ignoring all the strife
That fills the world with lies, and boasts
Of pain and anguish 'till, at the most,
We scream our souls down into hell.

Abhorring beauty, now we fell
The lovely tree. We cannot bear
The thought that something living there
Could be at peace. The world must know
Our pain, *our* loss, *our* manufactured woe.

I think that I shall never hear
A poem like Kilmer's ever again.

Typer's Block

I have a song in my heart
That won't come out my fingers
So, you don't get to hear it.

Ode to My Cat

Why does *oi;* my cat *kjn'o* like to help me? *kij*
When I am writing *lkn* poetry?
*s*He hunts and pecks among the keys
And purrs *wx* to show me how he's pleased

If I don't get th*j*e words just right
He calmly types *";lknkl ;lk wo;id ite"*
He's honed his craft. *lokj* His gift sublime
doth color *jik* every single line.

Why does my *!# cat like to help me?
He sees potential and if he *dfas*
hdgf Could give his talent onto me
I'd understand his poetry. *o;aijd;las*

This poem was a challenge to myself. I love patterns and wanted to see if I could write with the strict rule that the number of syllables in each line must progress from the beginning to the middle in increasing odd numbers (1,3,5,7,9,11). Then turn and run down to the end with even numbers (12,10,8,6,4,2).

I though about it for a while and gave up, moved to my bedroom and started to make the bed. Who knew a mussed bed could be my muse?

Odds and Evens

Chores.
What a bore.
Can't think of a more
Wretched thing that I abhor.
I'll get on a train to Baltimore.
I'll change into a big, ancient brontosaur
And trample on my room until it ain't no more,
But then my mom will be extremely sore,
And I will have to answer for
The mess about the floor.
I can't ignore
My chores

A couple of days off with nothing to do is an invitation for silliness. Everything in my house seemed to speak poems to me. So, here's a peak inside an idle mind.

The Litter Box

The litter box
Give me the jitters box
The little critter emitter box
The sausage and fritter box
The clump and s#!tter box
Give it to my sister box
Need a bigger box
Or a few less cats

Unrequited Love

I'm ready to go,
but Puddin' has come to share my space.
Got places to go,
but he purrs when he looks at my face.
Gotta get gone,
Oh, just one more scratch behind his ear.
Clocks tickin' on
but he's so soft, and I fear
I'm lost in love for my Puddin'.
A love that is surely endurin' the test of time.
Oh, love sublime.
Until the chime of a can opening.
He's off and running.
Oh, love how fickle, how callous and hard;
That he would eschew it and show no regard
for me.
He'd sell me downriver
For a bowl of chopped liver.

Ode to a Pen

Have you considered the marvel of a pen?
You pick it up. A useless thing, but when
You click the top the point appears.
The ink supply might last for years.
And when you're done you click again.
It hides its point within the den
of secrets, springs, and ink galore
Until you want to write some more.

An Ode to An Ode

The Title is the thing I struggle with the most
I finish a poem that I want to post
But the "title" box stops me in my tracks.
It's not the words I lack
But the essence of the work needs to be
Encapsulated in the title, you see.
I'm stumped, harrumph, and rar, rar,rar
I sit and I stew for half-a-year
Until it occurs to me, "Here's a solution."
"I'll call it an ode." Oh, what elocution!

How the World Spins

I know a man
Who thinks he can
Do whatever he wants.
He lifts his nose
And spouts some prose
He believes he's some kind of savant.
I've spent some time
To know his mind
I find it too small and perverse.
He speaks with a smile
But his thoughts are vile
And self-centered. There is nothing worse.

I know a woman
Who thinks she knows more than
The rest of humanity's kind.
She pontificates
While everyone waits
To hear the small thought from her mind.
I've wasted time
Trying to find
An idea not small and obtuse.
She speaks like a child
And waves her hands wild
And thinks she is really abstruse.

I know one below,
(Me, if you must know),
The heavens who fathoms deep thought.
A creative and smart one
Whose mind is a fine-spun
Arrangement of truths some have sought.
I'm aware those around me
Are trapped there below me.
I have much advice I can give them.
If they would just listen
They'd grasp what they've missed of
My thoughts and my gifts and my wisdom.

Writer’s Block

Well, here I am
Nothing to write
Nothing comes to mind

Just a wasteland where thoughts used to live.

I’m in a jam.
I’ll type in spite
of my dearth of line.

But my mind has no musings to give.

Writer’s block.
Not an original thought.
The reason for all of our woes.

It’s plagued scribes from the beginning of time

I can’t unlock
the big Pandora’s box
That traps writers’ musings and prose.

The key would be worth a lifetime of rhyme.

The Price of Progress

I could walk a mile and never see more than my imagination.
A walk of two would still not exceed man's dreams of machination.
Earth groans under man's need.

Mankind has redefined the land and sea
to accommodate our vision of paradise. A stack of brick and steel.
Our towers of Babel, Incisions that puncture the sky.

There's hardly a place where you don't see
preparation for a build. Power lines, homes, and fallen trees,
A monument to nature killed.

I don't know why we believe our works are more
beautiful and divine than what earth was created for.
Love God's, not man's, design.

Come Dream With Me

I have read poems about dreaming
I have sung songs about scheming
"Come dream with me" they say
"I will take you away
To a land where dreams come true."
I don't want to come with you.

How about you come with me
Into a world of fantasy?
A world where limits are unknown
And only my imagination claims the throne
Of the world's desires.
Let *my* dreams inspire.. . .

We'll drive down a pink road
In a pink car with a pink toad
And we're picked up by a giant pink rabbit
Who seems to pick up cars as a habit.
We're now on his shoulder and he gives us a pat
That makes all the tires bounce and then go flat.

We’re flying through air
With the greatest of ease
But there is no net
And no swinging trapeze.
We laugh with delight as we fall (We’re not lookin’)
And splat in a big bowl of soft chocolate puddin’.

Or how ‘bout a sail on a sea of blue grass
And we find ourselves stuck in a squishy morass
Of blue mud and blue rocks and blue crocodile teeth
That chomp on our boat from above and beneath.
But as jaws chomp again, we jump up like a flash
And run for the shore across blue spik-ed backs.

Don’t give me your rainbows and castles and roses.
I want some adventure and thrills. A few doses
Of unicorn dreams will be all I can stand.
But give me a trip into space in a can
Of sweet pickle relish. That’s all that I need.
You come dream with *me*. It’s fun guaranteed.

A Collection of Limericks

I've sat at my desk now all day
To try and find beauty to say
I think of a word
And make it absurd
Like sumthing or pensill or twoday

A chair sits alone in a room
Through daylight and twilight and gloom
It never complains
Although it restrains
From ever escaping its tomb.

Consider the cat who's asleep
On a soft blanket. All in a heap.
His legs are akimbo.
His head upside down. Though
He'll lay there and not make a peep.

Since when did my muscles get stiff?
I rise from each chair with a "hfff."
My knees started creaking.
My back is mistreating
me. How did I end up like this?

A purr is a cat's perfect song
So, let them sing. What could go wrong?
Although a meow
Can turn to a howl
The neighbors can hear 'cross the lawn.

I met a man riding a pony;
His angry face like pepperoni.
His horse did a tumble
and I heard him mumble
"A ride on a horse is baloney"

I've heard people say that time flies.
And spinach can help body size.
If spinach and time
could their talents combine
Then big bodied old folks would fly.

Rhythm Woes

If all the poems in all the world were written by my teacher,
They all would be, (Oh woe is me), iambic pentameter.
The sing-song nature of the line just makes her heart a-twitter,
She swoons and leans upon her desk like Cupid's arrow hit her.
I'll never understand the way she hangs on every word.
The sing-song nature of the lines to me is quite absurd.
Can we not say a line or two in syllables of twenty?
Or maybe in a meter that adjusts to few or plenty?
But no. We live inside the rhythm of this wretched beat for
I study poems from one who loves iambic pentameter.

To See God

I wonder at my great God
How awesome is He
The God who created all

Sees the smallness of beings
Wandering the earth
And He loves us all to death.

The Sunrise

The sun rises.
Low light creeps over the horizon
And shades the sky with orange hues.
The promise of day, but not quite the end of night.

The sun rises.
And a line of light turns dark to shade
And shade to a light that blinds.
The entrance of day, The loss of night.

The sun rises.
A fleeting moment when light meets dark,
Not as enemies, but a changing of the guard.
Day takes his post and light commands the earth.

My father waged a mighty battle against Alzheimer's. The last three years of his life he lived with me. Our shared love of music brought us close throughout my life. Our shared love for my son drew us even closer. To care for him in his need was a no-brainer.

For three years we lived life together, but the last one proved too much for him. He had always been loving, but stoic. He kept his calm even in the storm. I watched him spiral down into oblivion: couldn't read, couldn't talk, blown into intense emotion by the winds of events around him.

The hardest days came to be the ones when he didn't recognize me. He would smile at my attentiveness, but the fact that I was his daughter and we had shared a life together had escaped his mind. The pain of that reality was more difficult than his death.

It's been a few years and grief has given way to a certainty that debilitating disease is evil; a scourge only God can wipe away. Too many people know what I'm talking about, and too many people don't. Either way, here's a glimpse of the mended tatters of my experience.

Relentless

I loved you when your energy
Was unstoppable. Young and free
You moved through life with graceful form,
Unaware of the coming storm.

And when you slowed, I loved you still.
Determination moved your will.
You pushed your body past its prime
Denying you'd run out of time.

Your mind became your enemy
But you fought back and held at bay
The fatal spiral down to loss
Of self, of joy, of pain and thought.

And now I look into your eyes
And know that you don't recognize
The one who's loved you all this time.
The final pain of loss is mine.

Oh, time that steals our summer days
And brings the winter, cold with age.
You spurn love's hope. Our days you take
And leave the wreckage of heartache.

The Problem with Sayings

To talk your ear off would deny
All future conversation (sigh)
You'd see mouths move from up to down
But ears detached don't give you sound.

And why would people shoot the breeze?
A waste of bullets. Just shoot cheese
Or baggies, that's less of a mess.
A silly thought I must confess.

I understand a house on fire
Would make you run fast as required.
But why the smiles if all is burned?
Best leave the matches undisturbed.

Why does a frog live in your throat?
Or does he visit? Maybe float
Among the mucus with his young.
Tadpoles who'll live under your tongue.

You kick the bucket and you die.
It's too extreme. I don't know why
You only cry when milk is spilled,
But kick the bucket and you're killed.

“I’ve got the blues” not greens or yellows?
A nice, pale shade of purple mellows.
Why can’t we have the pinks or whites?
To stick with blue doesn’t seem right.

I’ll take a walk up on cloud nine,
And wonder if cloud ten combines
With nine and gives me much more room.
But God, I don’t want to presume.

To play your heart strings would require
A doctor and a cut most dire.
I’m not sure I would want to play
your heart that much, I’m sad to say.

Now who would go down in the dumps?
It’s smelly, rotten, full of bumps
Of who know what?! I can’t believe
That people would be so naïve.

This language that we use today
Makes no darn sense and doesn’t say
What we express. If man would use
Plain words, I’d go over the moon!

My faith in God who lived, died, and rose for us, sustains all I am. This requires participation in the community of saints. However, I find many doctrines lead to childish beliefs. This "church" (the bride of Christ) seems to forget who she belongs to and what we are created for. We are to do great things in the world, not hide behind our walls or think about Jesus only on Saturday night or Sunday morning. Laodicea waits for those who don't embrace His truth.

Wake, Bride, and Live

How can we be ignorant of another's pain?
Can we chose to turn away and remain
True to any ideals we hold dear?
Do we live the gospel so the world can hear
The strains of grief Jesus groaned on the cross?

Should we treat His death so cavalier
That those near us living lives of fear
Stay in bondage when we refuse to pray?
"There's time enough to pray," we say.
Dare we spit on the life that Jesus lost?

The sheep of Jesus languish in the fold,
Too scared or tired to give Him to the world,
And wolves come in to tell us, "It's alright.
The Kingdom is for you. No need to fight.
The blood He shed for you is only dross."

We are the church that is to be His bride.
What bride is this, bruised and unsanctified?
We chose to greet offense as an old friend
While the offender bleeds in shame again.
Is this the bride for whom He paid such cost?

The Spirit grieves to be let loose from us.
His power wasted while we prune and fuss
To make ourselves seem beautiful in our eyes,
And hide the filth inside He will despise.
His power and authority we've lost.

Oh, martyrs' blood, cry out from the cold ground
And move our hearts to scream, "We can't be bound
By fear and laziness. Our lover waits.
Wake soul. Wake spirit. Be what He creates.
A one on fire with love and clinging to the cross.

I will enfold your pain into my arms.
I will speak truth to those who mean me harm.
I will not shrink from speaking out His name
and tell the world He came to life again.
Oh, Holy Lord, Your light shine at all cost.

I must confess, I have been married twice. Both ended in failure. I've no desire to try again, not because I have no faith in myself, but because I prize the depth that comes from a shared history and now, I'm too old to create one with someone I learn to love.

However, I observe happy couples around me who have achieved this lauded goal and am encouraged to know it's possible, and wonderful, and "deeper than the ocean" kind-of magnificent. Through the years, when it works, its amazing.

Observation is a shallow experience, but here is my homage to history-making people.

True Strength

I sing a song of the sons of men
Who strive to reach new heights and win.
The strength of man is in his fight.
Life beats him down, but it's his rite
Of passage. The bitter night
Of trial that brings a better life.

I sing of woman who through the ages,
With stalwart heart her battle wages.
Love is her strength and her foundation.
The strongest rock. The purest passion.
She knows the cost of disconnection
And seeks to heal life's devastation.

Each one is mighty in their right.
Each one will claim a vict'ry, but
The victory will be much more sweet
When they, together, each complete.
He sharpens her. She sharpens he.
And find their true strength lies in "we"

Judge Not

I sit on a park bench and watch people walk by
Living their lives, unaware that I
Study them.

A man dressed in rags stumbles by with a bag
In his hand. He falls into a doorway, ragtag,
Drinking gin.

The stench of him causes a woman to cross the road.
Her perfect dress and shoes strode carefully to
Avoid sin.

My thoughts now turn to gratitude
I'm not that man, or the woman who'd
Reject him.

What causes us to judge another's life?
To say, "There but for the grace of God go I."
Why not us?

I am called to find love for this woman and man
It's not a feeling, but a choice that I can
Make or not.

And as I contemplate these higher thoughts of compassion
Pride stirs in me. A self-serving woman of action,
I choose love.

All of the judgements I made on my bench now haunt me.
There go I. Would God ever want someone like me to
Do His will?

If I am to love the woman and man, then I must love
myself as well.
That is the hardest love of all. I know where sin inside me
dwells
And I'm shamed.

I take my soul in hand and love myself like Jesus can.
Repentance leads to joy. My eyes see the pain the man's
Running from.

The woman's revulsion now seems to me to be her fear
Of rejection. Social standards tell her that she
Must look good.

The ragged man, the perfect one, they both are living a life
Of lies and hidden wounds, but God gives them His light
Of mercy.

Shouldn't we?

I Don't Want to Work

I don't want to work today
I'm tired. I don't know what to say.
There're papers all over my desk.
I'm sleepy. I'll just take a rest.
A man is standing at the door.
He needs to sell a humidor.
I've got a list of things to buy.
Won't be a minute. Gotta fly.
That show about that world war battle
Is finally on the History Channel.
Mom, may I play VR instead?
Or can I please just stay in bed?
"Get out of bed and stop your whine.
For goodness sake. You're thirty-nine!"

Sleepless Night

I know some folks
Who like to toast
Their lives with mugs of beer
They stumble round
All over town
To bring us all some cheer.

They're happy drunks
But a short dunk
In water, cold and deep
Would quiet down
The stupid clowns
Who sing away my sleep.

Turn About is Fair Play

Love of my life, oh, be my wife and we'll be filled with joy.
"No."
A girl for you and just for me a bouncing baby boy.
"No."
Can I tell you that I love you just to make you smile?
"No."
My love burns brighter even when rejection is my trial.
"No"
Oh, my love, do you not know how much you make me grieve?
"No."
You give me hope. We can elope, my spicy jalape
"No,"
You'll wed me while you ride upon a silver palomi
"No."
And every morning you could fix us cups of cappucci
"No"
We'd honeymoon in luxury atop a huge volca
"No"
And I would sing a bass to your so lyric soprani
"No"
Oh love, my joy, my beauty, my inspiring andanti
"No."
Our love will light the world more than a bright, blazing infer
"No."

How Would it Be?

How would it be if I flew up high
And touched the sky? or maybe I
Could run like a cheetah at speeds quite fast.
Be on time at last. That'd be a blast.

I wonder what it would be like to see
A bumblebee as big as me.
Would it find flowers to light upon?
They'd have to weigh almost a ton.

I like to think my imaginings
Are mindless whims, just silly things,
But suffering thrives all the world around
And silly thoughts drive out the sound of it.

In quiet drops it fills the ground
With blood from wounds inflicted on us.
"Why must we suffer thus?" I say,
As heartbreak turns my eyes away.

What if I grew wings and flew up high?
I'd rise to heights where I'd deny
The torments of this blackened home.
It's all too much to face alone.

Can we find peace within the fight?
Put down our weapons and unite
ourselves against our enemies.
I'll strengthen you. You strengthen me.

We'll face the whole world, you and me.
And drive back pain and suffering.
The sun will rise on our great nation
Alas, that's my imagination
Again.

Q and A

Q: Why do poems have to rhyme?
If we just took a little time
We find some other words to fit
The pattern of our thoughts a bit.

I'm not complaining. Oh, not me.
But if I write some poetry
It's difficult to be restrained
Inside a rhythm. What is gained

From toiling under heavy chains
Of metered verse and rhymed refrains?
Let poets everywhere come see
The beauty of a word that's free.

A: But that is what the world calls prose.
This simple fact everyone knows.
You take away the rhyme and verse
And that will grieve the universe.

Who'll speak of stars that shine above?
Or languish in the throes of love?
When heartache overtakes my peace,
What, but a poem, can grief release?

Q: But I want to speak out my mind
And chains of rhythm will entwine
My thoughts before I get them out.

A: Then write a book, you great big lout!

I read a poem by a wonderful young poet (Harry Baker. I highly recommend him) who rhymed about Christmas's past. I enjoyed the poem and thought, *I've seen a lot more Christmas's than he has. Shouldn't I write down some worldly wisdom of my own?*

I gave it a moment's thought (which you will deduce as you read) and wisdom poured freely from my mind. You know, the wisdom you get after you've made that decision you regret as soon as you start.

By-gone Years

In all the years I've been alive
(I'm facing birthday sixty-five)
I never thought myself as old,
But now it's coming I am told.

When young, my parents set the rules
My life restricted by their school
Of right and wrong, play and song
My own thoughts were rebellion.

I grew up, as we all do,
I won't review those years for you.
We all live lives of loss and joy
And work we'd rather not employ.

The years go by (and by and by)
Until one day you realize
The woman in the mirror there
May just be you with graying hair.

But mentally I find that I
Still think that I am twenty-nine.
I have a thought, “That’s good!” I think
“I’ll fix the dripping kitchen sink.”

I rise from position supine
And find I can’t straighten my spine.
No problem. I just need a moment
To check each disk and spine component.

Slowly I straighten up my back
And heave a sigh after a crack
Or two. Now I’m arranged
to tackle any challenge made.

Upon my toolbox I advance
I’ll not leave anything to chance.
The wrench I choose will do the trick
This job will be done in a jiff.

I open up the cupboard door
And drop my body on the floor.
My legs regret my energy.
My back begins to worry me.

“Eventually, I’ll get back up.”
“But how?” (My back is speaking up.)
“I’ll grab the countertop and pull.”
“Don’t count on me, you big numskull,”

And now my legs start to complain.
"How will you get us up again?"
"Well, it's your job to raise me up."
"Not when your up is that far up."

So here I am upon the floor
Before an open cupboard door
Thinking my body young and fine
Like I remembered twenty-nine.

Now I must take myself in hand
And find some courage to withstand
The loud complaints, the groan and creak
Of old bones rising on old feet.

The wrench feels heavy in my hand
And now that I can finally stand
I wisely put the wrench away
"I'll fix the sink another day."

The couch on which I laid supine
Will soothe my legs, my back align.
And as I lay my weary head
Upon the cushion, soft and red

I think, "That's quite enough for me,
I'll rest and save my energy
Tomorrow seems the perfect time."
Just like I thought at twenty-nine.

About the Author

Joy is from Hampton, Virginia. She grew up the youngest child of a family of five. Her father was the Director of Music at the First United Methodist Church in a historical building over 200 years old. She has fond memories of her father tickling the keys of the pipe organ. She continued in his footsteps gaining a love for music. It has become her life. She has a Batcher of Music Education from James Madison Univ. and a Master of Music from Northern Arizona University. Poetry has the same appeal because of the same rhythms and meters.

She has discovered she loves poetry as much as music (even if it is just silliness).

email: joynoel57@gmail.com

website: quillonfire.com

www.ingramcontent.com/pod-product-compliance
Lightning Source LLC
LaVergne TN
LVHW020528160826
845677LV00015B/3969

* 9 7 9 8 3 6 6 5 0 6 4 8 9 *